Newmarket Public

EARTHWO
UNLIMIT

EARTHWORMS UNLIMITED

BACKYARD EARTHWORM BREEDING

Amy Brown

Kangaroo Press

Cover illustration by Katie Ravich

Drawings courtesy of Chris, Kate and Sarah Blenkinsopp

© Amy Brown 1994

Reprinted 1995
This edition published in 1994 by Kangaroo Press Pty Ltd
3 Whitehall Road Kenthurst NSW 2156 Australia
P.O. Box 6125 Dural Delivery Centre NSW 2158
Printed by Australian Print Group, Maryborough Vic 3465

ISBN 0 86417 631 7

*This book is dedicated
with affection
to all the worms
I have handled . . .
and a few others I have known!*

Acknowledgment

The author gratefully acknowledges David R. Lambert's permission to include material from his book *Earthworm Breeding for Profit*.

Contents

Foreword

Gardeners who want to improve and subsidise their passion for planting, small landholders, alternative lifestylers, fish and bird breeders take note! Breeding earthworms will cost you little, take minimal time, and will help make ends meet. Becoming a commercial earthworm breeder is a different matter, but still shouldn't cost the earth!

I started a small earthworm farm because a relative planning to return from overseas needed work, which, at the time was almost impossible to find. I had a long-standing interest in earthworms and had been fascinated to read about worm farms in the USA, especially the work of Charlie Morgan and Earl B. Shields. Undaunted by my ignorance, and without consulting the relative, I decided an earthworm farm would provide him with an interesting and profitable small business, and me with some superannuation money.

I read all I could find about earthworms, which, short of Charles Darwin's treatise *The Formation of Vegetable Mould through the Action of Worms* (published in 1881), wasn't much. It became clear that setting up a small experimental earthworm farm was the only way to learn. In another age it used to be called 'on the job training'! I took 1400 earthworms out of a relative's compost, and set up a crude ground bed in my backyard, two hours away from my job, intending to take a somewhat detached view of the proceedings.

My detachment vanished when the earthworms began to multiply! No time for such a luxury when I was counting worms, making bedding, hefting boxes and taking notes, in between driving up and down to my demanding job in Auckland. To top it off, the relative didn't return. Despite this I experimented and learned a phenomenal amount about the tough and durable little earthworm.

If you're a potential earthworm breeder or a keen gardener I know this book will provide some of the information you will need to try your hand at earthworm breeding. I haven't tried everything I've read and written about, but I have left out anything I considered to be useless or unnecessary information. This book should help you avoid some of my mistakes. Not least of all, I hope the book will help you enjoy and respect the amazing earthworm.

Background

Earthworms have long been recognised for the benefits they bring to the soil. The Pharaohs of ancient Egypt were amongst the first people to recognise the importance of earthworms and instigated further study by a section of the priesthood. In fact they were considered so indispensible to the agricultural economy that Cleopatra declared the earthworm sacred and anyone trying to take them out of the country was subjected to the death penalty. However, it wasn't until the nineteenth century when Charles Darwin undertook a 70-year study of earthworms that we gained our first real understanding of these small creatures.

Nowadays, agriculturalists, soil scientists, environmentalists, rubbish disposal experts, and gardeners of all kinds value these humble creatures. However care must be taken that the correct earthworm for the task be used. There is some confusion over how suitable the (mainly) commercially produced species (known as composters) are in the improvement of agricultural soils. Unless quantities of rich organic material are available or can be added, agricultural soils need to be stocked or replenished with soil-dwelling earthworking species (known as earthworkers) which produce at a slower rate in the less organically rich soil. This book deals mainly with composting worms.

In the USA, Canada and Japan, composting worms are used in many tip sites to accelerate decomposition of organic waste and to generate profits through the sale of worm castings—the nutrient-rich excreta. The success of such enterprises has shown that 'rubbish in' equals saleable 'worm compost out'.

Increasingly, worm castings are being used to promote plant growth in pastures, orchards and gardens. Research and experiments have shown that earthworm castings contain approximately five times more available nitrogen, seven times more available phosphorus, three times more exchangeable magnesium, one and a half times more calcium and eleven times more available potassium than ordinary top soil. When using castings in the garden you can be assured your plants are receiving a safe, organic fertiliser which is free of chemical pollutants.

As well as disposing of rubbish, providing rich, inexpensive compost, and improving the soil, earthworms should be looked at as a way of making money. Even a small farm in the backyard has the potential to tap into the growing demand for earthworms.

A Little Terminology

Aerating the beds Loosen the top 100 cm of beds monthly to air the bedding and prevent packing down of material.

Casts/castings Mineral-rich piles of digested and decayed worm excreta, pH7 (neutral).

Dividing beds and boxes Divide half the bedding including worms and capsules and spread it to half-fill a new bed. Spread out the remainder in the original bed. Top up both beds with new bedding.

Limestone (calcium carbonate) Lime helps to dissipate harmful acids which form in the bedding and settle to the bottom of the bed. Decomposed granite, crushed oyster or other calciferous shells can also be used to raise the pH level.

Migrating, crawling, wandering Continuous wet weather, overcrowding, and dislike of food encourages worms to leave home. Water in the mornings—not late afternoon, and mulch 5 cm away from bed edges to discourage travel. Large farms use perimeter lights to prevent wandering.

Mulch A heavy layer of organic refuse which slowly decays on the soil surface, protecting soil and organisms from the harmful effects of sun, rain, wind and snow. Mulch helps water absorption, reduces runoff and erosion, and shelters and feeds earthworms. Mulch includes straw, dead weeds, old manure, fine shells, leaves, grass clippings, shredded paper, cardboard, carpet and underfelt.

pH A measure of the soil ranging from acid (4 or 5), through neutral (7), to alkaline (8 or 9). Worms like to live in neutral soil. To change acid towards neutral, sprinkle garden lime. To change alkaline towards neutral, add peat moss or shredded newsaper.

Pit-run worms A mixture of worms of all sizes in the bed, from eggs through to mature breeders.

Rubbish or garbage All organic waste including meat, cooked or uncooked vegetable and fruit peelings, old coleslaw, the remains of children's dinners, cooking disasters, tea leaves or bags, coffee grounds, vacuum cleaner dust, old cotton or wool waste, dryer lint, cooking oil, crushed egg shells, cat bounty (i.e. dead mice, rats and birds), mower-slashed garden weeds, soaked torn up cardboard boxes, shredded paper, torn newspaper, lawn clippings, juicer waste . . . earthworms will eat almost anything that has lived and died.

Watering Water gently through a fine spray to keep beds damp but crumbly. A drier or damper cycle will stimulate breeding. Don't wet surrounding areas as it encourages inquisitiveness.

Worms! Who Cares?

Earthworms will bring these benefits to your garden:

- They oxygenate the soil and improve water retention by pulverising soil and creating tunnels in their search for food. Earthworm tunnels may be easily seen, especially when forking through dry soil.
- They hasten the breakdown of organic waste.
- They incorporate organic waste directly into the soil in the form of rich castings which are immediately available for use by plants.
- They reduce the need for sometimes dubious and usually expensive chemical fertilisers.
- They are able to transform tonnes of organic waste into rich compost to use in and on the soil and in plant pots.
- They are wonderful converters of orchard waste and can help prevent the spread of fungal diseases.

Keen observers will notice an occasional abundance of worms around plant roots. This does not mean that the worms are eating your precious plants, but is a sign of the symbiotic relationship which exists between plants and worms. The worms deposit fertile castings around the roots which enhance plant growth and in return the plants secrete a substance which the worms seem to find desirable.

Worms prefer to live in fertile soil. They seek out and eat the organic riches available in the soil and repay the favour by excreting their rich deposits directly in the soil.

Throwing a handful of worms on a clay bank will do nothing for either the clay or worms, but dig down 30 or 40 cm, add some organic waste, dampen, add worms, and they will have a base to work from.

Kitchen waste, excluding meat and fish scraps and old smelly cheese, can be buried under the top 10 cm of soil or covered with a mulch of hay, straw, pine needles or newspapers.

One way of providing sustenance to tired fruit trees or shrubs is to spread a container of kitchen waste near the roots of the tree, cover the scraps with layers of newspaper, water thoroughly and then cover with a spadeful or two of soil or compost. Earthworms will do the rest, stimulating and rejuvenating the trees into healthy new growth.

This very superior way of mulching gives the worms a protected environment and your plants the benefit of retained moisture. As with all mulches, weeds are discouraged and the worms are protected sufficiently to get on with the job they love to do. Much of the work of cultivating and fertilising can be left to them, leaving you free to plant or harvest, or even read a book.

Giving the worms favourable conditions to live in will encourage them to set up house in your garden. Your recompense will be fewer weeds, healthier plants and flavoursome, truly organic vegetables which are safe from dangerous pesticides.

Profit or Pleasure?

Getting Started

Only you can decide whether your earthworm venture will be one of profit or pleasure. It could be a hobby farm which will not only improve your soil by utilising garden and household waste, but also educate the children (or grandchildren) and provide the neighbours with a new talking point. It could be a part-time job which will benefit other gardens in the district as well as your pocket, or it could be a full-time business which should bring you profitable returns and provide an ecological boost to the environment.

Whatever you decide, start on a scale you can maintain and afford. Be modest in your approach. Experiment with a planned compost heap, a mini worm farm in a rubbish bin or old bathtub, or a few propagation boxes until you have an understanding of the worms, their feed, their bedding, their growth, their reproductive cycle and so on.

Even if your goal is to run and own the biggest commercial earthworm farm in the country, start small so that any errors you make won't lose you money before you've earned any. That means either raiding someone's compost bin or buying stock. It also means providing containers or beds to put the stock in. (See Worm Bodes)

Planning the Project

A few basic rules will make your project easier to handle.

1. Read as much as possible about worms. Libraries are a good starting point although they have few up-to-date books about the subject. Charles Darwin's book on earthworms makes for dry reading! You may find the reading list at the end of the book helpful.

2. Ask questions. If I had a dollar for every minute I've spent answering questions about earthworms I'd have a healthier bank balance, but I haven't minded. Gardeners and worm fanciers are almost always nice to talk to.

3. Decide what you want to achieve. Is this for fun, for education, or for profit? Set goals!

4. If the goal is to return money, prepare a small business plan, however basic. If you need to borrow money to get started you'll find most banks uncooperative. Look at local enterprise schemes. Could this be a cooperative effort? Are there like-minded people prepared to put in a few dollars each, either in cash or kind? Or do you have you a rich relative?

5. Set out on paper first exactly what you will need—bins, containers, cartons. Where can you get free feed or material to make bedding? Are you near stables where manure and straw might be available? Do you live near a food processing plant or a sewage treatment station? Are you near a beach where seaweed is tossed up after storms? Is there a pig farm nearby where you can buy slurry?

Become familiar with your local recycling tip. Potential worm bins may be available for free, not to mention wood planks for raised beds, wooden boxes for propagation boxes, and cardboard boxes for food and bedding.

6. Check out your resources, look at the project again and finally decide whether you can handle anything bigger than a compost area or mini-bed to provide for your own needs. Do you really want to make money? How do you feel about handling worms?

You've made the decision to go ahead? Great! Your whole life has just changed and you will now spend your time looking for endless supplies of earthworm food and bedding. In return, your earthworms will repay your interest and investment with rich compost, productive gardens, and money—maybe a lot, depending on your perseverance and your goals. You won't need to spend sleepless nights counting sheep. You can count worms instead! Just joking! You will almost certainly weigh your worms, not count them.

One other point! If you own spades, shovels or other sharp implements which will cut worms in half, either get rid of them or put them at the back of the garden shed. Spades are definitely not suitable! Buy good quality garden forks, both the hand and foot variety, and a three-tined, long-handled fork for turning bedding. Contrary to popular belief, the way to increase worm production is not to cut them in half. While the front end may survive to grow a new tail, both ends will not regenerate.

The only other implements you really need at this stage are a large sack of garden lime, a good wheelbarrow, a pH meter to test the acidity of the bed or bin, and maybe a device to measure the temperature in bedding and compost. (I haven't got one. I still stick my hand in.)

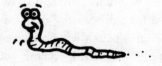

Who Needs Worms?

Every gardener and garden needs worms ... as well as agriculturalists, horticulturists, food processors, bait sellers, and people in a host of other occupations.

Primary Markets for Worms

Gardeners Earthworms service the life support systems of plants, converting dead and dying organic matter into rich plant food.

Householders and flat dwellers Worms can be used as an organic waste disposal system, converting waste to fertiliser in both town and country.

Poultry, game-bird and bird breeders Worms are a valuable food supplement, and turn waste into profit.

Aquariums, trout hatcheries, tropical and goldfish breeders Worms are easily digested by all kinds of exotic fish and may be fed live.

Eel farmers and exporters Worms are a favoured food of eels.

Zoos Fish and caged and enclosed birds thrive on nourishing worm protein.

Rabbit, emu and ostrich farmers Worms may be kept under rabbit hutches to clean up and convert rabbit manure into valuable compost.

Pig and dairy farmers Enormous quantities of slurry waste are cleaned and converted by worms, providing high protein meal for cattle and pigs.

Orchardists Worms till the soil around trees without disturbing root systems, providing better drainage and decreasing root rot. They provide fertile castings to rootlets and reduce fungal diseases by eating rotting leaves, fruit and fungal spores. They are wonderful for rejuvenating old trees.

Breeding worms for other worm farmers Small growers can fill big growers' overflow orders when demand is high.

Laboratories Worms can be used not only as food for experimental animals but also as a waste converter.

Fishermen Suitable for fresh and salt water fishing (but not trout), worms are the natural diet of fish. Live worms don't smell, are not wasted, and cost less than other types of bait.

Nurserymen and plant breeders Castings can be used in potting mixes and garden beds.

Food producers and processors, pulp and paper mills, produce markets, dairy and cheese factories Organic waste from these industries can be converted into profitable compost.

Farmers and pastoralists Earthworking worms help the transfer of decaying leaves, grasses and manures into plant foods below the soil surface. As the organic material breaks down, soil moisture retention is improved, thereby reducing the effects of low rainfall. Grass has greater nutritional value when worms are present. (See Pasture Growth Improvement)

Landscape gardeners Potential customers for worms, castings and capsules. Worms, once established beneath mulch and soil, service the plant systems providing improved soil nutrition, structure, aeration and water retention.

Sewage treatment plants Sewage sludge is excellent worm food and converts into rich fertile castings.

Local councils Tonnes of organic waste can be converted into saleable castings while increasing the life of rubbish tips.

Mining companies Earthworms can help in rehabilitating the stripped soil and tailings by creating new topsoil (providing organic matter is provided).

Secondary By-products

1. Potting soil or mulch from castings.
2. Potted plants for specialist markets, florists and export.
3. Vegetables.
4. Herbs and salad greens for restaurants, balcony gardeners.
5. Egg capsules for hobby or business.

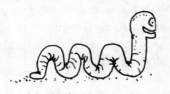

Pasture Growth Improvement from Earthworms

Research into the improvement and sustainability of pasturelands has demonstrated many benefits from the presence of earthworms. The basic benefits are that earthworking earthworms:

- cycle organic matter and prevent the accumulation of undecomposed organic matter on the soil surface;
- increase the soil porosity and water infiltration rate;
- increase the activity of microbes;
- improve the soil structure;
- increase pasture production;
- are able to incorporate lime and fertiliser into the soil.

Two current Australian projects sponsored by the Wool Research and Development Council (WRDC) have focused attention on earthworms and found a close link between earthworm populations and pasture productivity.

While earthworm specialists usually like to see about 400

earthworms/m^2, in the areas surveyed the populations were usually well below the levels needed to provide real benefits.

Researchers believe that some factors preventing the development of healthy earthworm populations are:

- Poor soil fertility, particularly low phosphorus content.
- Soil acidity. Some soils are naturally acidic, others have become acidic through the use of artificial fertilisers. Ammonium sulphate in fertilisers is toxic for worms, and a high copper content in the soil is also detrimental.
- Trampling by stock, especially at the higher stocking rates associated with block grazing.

Options for farmers who wish to increase earthworm populations, especially in drier areas include:

- Minimising soil disturbance.
- Spreading lime to raise the soil pH.
- Breaking up and spreading manure left by grazing animals. This makes it more readily available as an earthworm food.
- Deep ripping to remove compacted layers. Slashing or heavy strip grazing causes dieback of some roots which rot below the surface, providing tunnel space and rotting food for earthworms. If the field needs aerating, ploughing with disc or rotary hoes destroys the worms. Instead, strip-plough with a vibrating chisel plough. The earthworms are discouraged by a lot of noise so it's a good idea to limit the use of such machinery.
- Placing sod turf 10 cm deep in 30 cm squares from heavily populated worm areas. Set out at 6 metre intervals and sprinkle heavily with lime. Add more lime if the pH level warrants its use.

Any attempt to increase earthworm populations in pastures needs to take into account the different species present, the total mass of earthworms in each species, and variances in their behaviour.

Some burrow horizontally, never breaking the surface while others burrow vertically, and reach the surface regularly. Similarly, their breeding habits vary. The Night Crawler (*Lumbricus terrestris*) is known as the dew worm for its habit of breeding on the surface of dewy grass, while the Red worm (*Lumbricus rubellus*), a fast breeder, is more circumspect in its mating arrangements. The Field worm (*Aporrectodea caliginosa*) does not have the prolific breeding habits of the more gregarious Red worm, nor of the Manure worm (*Eisenia fetida*).

Field worms are a tremendous boost to an orchard. Transplant the worms in 30 cm x 30 cm square deep holes along the tree dripline, approximately eight holes per tree. Place 10 worms in each hole on top of a few centimetres of damp soil and compost. Fill in the holes loosely with soil and compost mix.

If you want to find Field worms, look for casts on the surface. You can encourage the worms to surface by watering heavily, or they can be collected in or after rainfall when the soil temperature is above 10°C. Playing fields or unsprayed lawns are a good place to look at night, and using a red filter over a torch will help you find them.

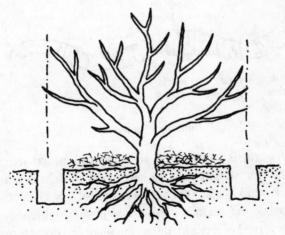

Worms give trees a boost

What is a Worm?

An earthworm is like a muscular doughnut-shaped tube composed of 90 to 150 segments, with a mouth at one end through which organic waste and soil enter, and an anus at the other end which is the exit for nutrient-rich castings. In between, the tube contains five hearts, a circulatory system, a digestive system, a mucous forming system, a brain and a nervous system. It also contains hundreds of nephridia—kidney-type organs, setae—retractable bristles in each muscular segment, male and female organs, calciferous glands for neutralising food, and a crop and gizzard with stones for grinding food.

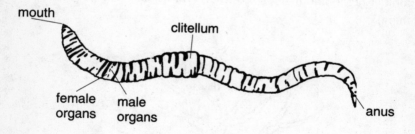

mouth

clitellum

female organs

male organs

anus

Anatomy of a worm

The earthworm is sensitive to light, vibration and temperature and it breathes through its skin. Its sensitivity to light is remarkable considering it lacks eyesight or visual nerves of any kind. It reacts to light by closing the surface capillaries through which oxygen is absorbed. Deprived of oxygen, the worm instinctively removes itself from the light source by burrowing downwards.

Casts are manufactured in the alimentary canal of the earthworm. Food is neutralised by constant additions of carbonate of lime secreted from the three pairs of calciferous glands near the gizzard. It is then finely ground prior to digestion.

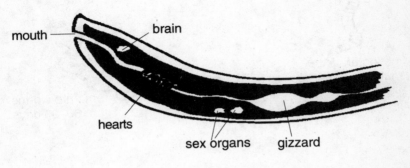

Cross-section of a worm

How They Reproduce and Reproduce and Reproduce

Earthworms are ready to breed when the 'saddle' or clitellum which is about one-third back from the mouth end, thickens, indicating maturity. This occurs normally between 60 and 90 days.

Earthworms are bi-sexual, but they must mate with another mature worm before they can perform both the male and female functions with which they are equipped.

It is a fascinating process to watch, although the time taken to complete the process (around 24 hours) is more exhausting for the watcher than the watched.

Head to tail, the two mature worms twist around each other in such a manner as to bring their clitellums into contact. Once each

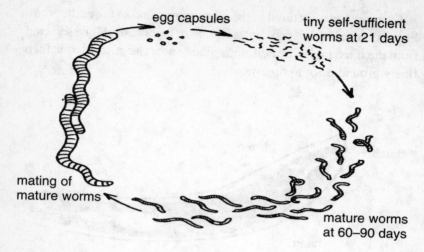

The breeding cycle

male cell has exchanged sperm to fertilise each other's female cells, the two worms separate.

Mucous is then secreted over the clitellum in a band, forcing the sperm and egg cells into contact. Once the band has fully formed, each worm slips itself backwards, removing the band over its head to form an egg or capsule. These capsules are a pale, lemon-coloured oval, similar to a teardrop in shape, and look like a small seed.

Each capsule lies in the soil for two to three weeks, depending on the weather and soil conditions, after which time the perfectly formed and self-sufficient baby earthworms hatch. The capsules may lie dormant for long periods of time, especially if produced before a spate of cold, inclement weather.

Although a capsule can yield up to twenty worms, in my role as voyeur I have never seen more then seven emerge. However, the newborn worms are so tiny it is possible I have miscounted.

Once maturity is reached, an active breeding worm, under favourable conditions—adequate food, moisture and temperature— will produce approximately 50 to 60 capsules per year—that is, about

200 young earthworms. The young worms themselves become breeders within three or four months, resulting in a rapid pyramiding of production within the year. An active breeding worm with its progeny is therefore capable of producing a 1000 to 1500 earthworms within a 12 month span.

Worms will limit their breeding to the available space and food. A smart worm fancier will continually expand the breeding space, but only if he or she needs the stock.

Common Worms

Of thousands of earthworm species four types are most commonly used to improve soil fertility.

The Night Crawler (*Lumbricus terrestris*), also known as the Dew worm, is about 12–15 cm long. It is a surface breeder which is commonly found in pastures in areas of high rainfall. Light grey to silver, thick and solid, it wriggles violently to escape ultraviolet light when brought to the surface.

The Field worm (*Aporrectodea caliginosa*) is redder and slightly smaller and generally remains below the surface. It is generally found in garden beds, lawns and paddocks.

Night Crawlers and Field worms are the best worms for revitalising lawn areas, paddocks and farmland, although neither species likes crowds. Ten worms in a 30 cm x 10 cm pad of turf constitutes a crowd.

The Red worm (*Lumbricus rubellus*) is 6–10 cm in length, red on top and sometimes paler and flatter underneath. It inhabits gardens, lawns, moist rotting compost heaps and leaf mould. They thrive anywhere there is moist organic material or soil covered with mulch.

They are far more gregarious than Night Crawlers and Field worms and will breed rapidly to fill the available bedding and food supply. Up to 5000 can inhabit a cubic foot in ideal conditions. They are ideal for gardens, lawns, and any organic waste disposal systems.

The Manure worm (*Eisenia fetida*), also commonly known as the Tiger worm, is similar to and as gregarious as the Red worm, but does not have the Red worm's flat pale underside. They have distinctive rings around the body, hence the name Tiger worm. They particularly like sloppy, manury conditions.

Worm fanciers and commercial growers generally have a mixture of Red worms and Manure worms as they basically do the same job, but this is not critical. Probably a sewage disposal project would do marginally better with more Tiger worms than Red.

Worms in Compost Beds

You can, of course, forget about a compost heap, buy worms and place them around plants in the garden, but they will do better in a controlled and contained environment.

Compost beds vary from the mouldering heap of lawn clippings and weeds variety, or expensive manufactured bins where the good stuff is always at the bottom, to smart two or three bin systems made of wood or concrete blocks. A little planning and preparation will reward you with a friendly environment for earthworms and litres of free rich compost and castings to use in the vegetable or flower garden. An added bonus will be thousands of earthworms to transplant directly into garden beds.

Ideally the compost area should be accessible, open to sunlight and shade, and not in the draughtiest corner of the yard. If starting a compost heap from scratch, try to have all the compostable material close to hand so you can build it in layers. It is a good idea to enclose the material on three sides if possible, and allow space for a further heap. My own area is very basic but suitable for my half-acre block— 2 m x 1.5 m divided in two and enclosed on three sides with corrugated iron.

Loosen the soil to a depth of about 10 cm. Add thick layers of coarse organic material like straw, hay, garden weeds (not oxalis or other noxious species) which have been chopped or clipped into small pieces, grass clippings, leaves (not too many at a time), torn newspaper, soaked ripped cardboard (worms love the glue), peat, or rinsed and chopped seaweed. Remember the trick of running your rotary mower over a pile of potential compost to shred it. Throw on a handful of lime to neutralise the pH.

Add a decent layer of manure, 100 cm or more if available. Horse, cow, rabbit, sheep or goat manures are good and commercially prepared sheep pellets are excellent. If using fresh horse manure, make sure the horses haven't been wormed recently. If they have, don't use the manure as the worming preparations may harm the earthworms. If you're adding fowl manure make sure it's aged and dry. If it's not aged, don't use too much as it can heat up and be too acidic for worms.

Throw on another handful of lime and add another decent layer of garden waste, straw, clippings, and so on. At this stage a layer of soil is a help. Add more manure if you have it, then more garden waste and lawn clippings.

If you do not have access to manure, use a mixture of soil, peat moss, shredded newspaper, torn up cardboard or shredded confidential documents which can be bought by the bail. Perhaps you have a friend who works in an office with a shredder. Soak the paper well before adding.

Now add kitchen or house waste, about a 40 cm layer. House waste includes vacuum cleaner dust, dog hair, dead houseplants, a little non-treated wood ash, and the feather pillow which burst, but not shiny, brightly coloured advertising brochures, especially ones with yellow or orange colouring. Throw on another handful of lime and a fine layer of soil over all the material. Wet the pile thoroughly, cover it with black plastic or polythene and weight it down.

After seven to ten days the pile will have warmed up and decomposed sufficiently to allow the introduction of the worms. About 500 are enough to start an average sized compost pit. Use more if they're available—the more the merrier and the faster the return of the compost. With any luck, earthworms already living in the ground underneath the heap will have been attracted by the delicious activity and will have already entered by stealth and occupied the heap.

The worms you have introduced will quickly settle and burrow into the bedding. Keep on placing kitchen and house waste on top as the worms will pull the food down from the surface. From time to time, lawn clippings and other garden waste can also be added to the pile. Cover the pile with wet sacks or shade cloth to exclude light and keep in the moisture.

In very cold and wet areas, you may need to place another cover of black polythene, corrugated iron or wooden boards over the pile to keep out excessive rain. In summer the pile must be kept damp. Old carpet is good for this purpose although the worms have a tendency to gather in carpet pile. Solution: turn the carpet pile face up.

Start compost area number two and perhaps concentrate this area on garden waste and clippings. The earthworm population won't be so high but heap one will be so full of worms you won't need to worry.

The upshot of all this activity is that more and more food will be consumed. Call on the neighbours for help, visit your local greengrocer for tired vegies, or add plenty of manure. At this stage you could think about taking a few thousand worms from the pile and placing them directly into the garden, but don't forget to provide a moist covering of mulch.

After several months have passed you will probably be one of those people who bore the pants off others by talking about their remarkable compost. Your edge will come by telling others how your compost was made entirely by worms. The decomposed organic material you used has become a rich, loamy, organically correct and environmentally suitable fertiliser for your house plants, vegetables, roses and so on. See how many other people you can turn on to worms!

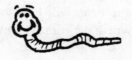

Garbage Guts

A Garbage Guts Muncher is a voracious consumer of organic material and a generous provider of worms. A Garbage Guts Muncher is a 'do-it-yourself' waste disposal unit which is noiseless, saves electricity, is guaranteed not to break down, is user and environmentally friendly and leaves you with rich compost and castings to use in the garden instead of wasting organic material down the drain.

The GGM can easily be set up using a bottomless slatted wooden box. Although the measurements are not critical, a box which is 125 cm wide and 125 cm high will hold kitchen waste from a large family.

A Garbage Guts Muncher is a voracious consumer of organic material and a generous provider of worms

1. Loosen and remove 10 cm of soil from where the box is to be positioned. Put the soil to one side. Set the box 10 cm into the ground to stop rats and mice gaining access. Add about 15 cm of chopped straw or hay mixed with some rough soil.

2. Collect your kitchen waste for a few days in a rubbish tin. Only use small amounts of citrus waste and onion skins, as these can be hard on the worms' digestive system.

3. When you have a decent amount—at least a third of the tin—spread the garbage can contents in the bottom of the box and cover with the 10 cm of soil you removed. Sprinkle a little lime over the top.

4. Empty around 4000 worms of mixed sizes on top of the soil and watch them burrow down. Ideally the area needs around 10 000 worms but 4000 will soon breed up.

5. Keep the contents damp but not sodden. Cover with a square of old carpet underfelt to keep in moisture and keep down smells.

6. Add the garbage daily or weekly with an occasional sprinkling of lime. Dampness, soil bacteria, micro-organisms and worms will convert garbage into black gold.

7. Once the box is full of compost and castings, feed the worms in one corner only as this will make it easier to fork them out to the next GGM location. Lift the box vertically into the new spot.

The compost and castings can be forked straight into garden beds or placed as a mulch around precious garden plants. To obtain a rich potting mix, combine the compost and castings with sand and/or peat moss.

Worm Bodes for Backyard Breeders

Whether you live in suburbia or 60 kilometres from the rural post pick-up, it should be possible within a short time to produce up to 50 000 worms a week. Sheds, basements, attics, garages, outbuildings, old barns, defunct plastic or glasshouses may all be converted to earthworm breeding areas.

Bins, Beds and Pits

Increasing earthworm production either for use in your own garden or on a commercial scale means removing them from their natural conditions and placing them in bins, beds or pits.

The easiest and cheapest way to get started is to use something adaptable, cheap, portable and preferably fairly durable. Wooden boxes or crates, old baths and laundry tubs, washing machine bowls,

A worm bed in an old bath

water tanks, empty oil drums, discarded refrigerators, even television carcasses might be pressed into service for your first bin/s.

A bin may be a tin can or a specially constructed box, portable only when empty. A bed or pit may be a hole in the ground, concrete blocks, metal tanks, or wooden or ceramic structures containing many hundreds of cubic feet of compost or bedding.

Whatever your bins or beds are made of do not invest more than you can afford. Think about it! Can you make the structure you were about to buy? Is there something cheaper you could use, free from the recycling section of the tip, for example. Frankly, the worms won't complain about their housing unless they're waterlogged, their beds are acidic or the food is not to their liking.

Indoor Beds

Indoor beds or pits can be built from rough timber, concrete blocks, small tanks, plastic containers, whatever. A plastic rubbish bin with holes punched in the base, set on small blocks above a drainage tray provides an economical and simple mini worm farm. Wooden pits or bins should be built a few inches above the floor, not only for

An indoor bed constructed from timber

timber preservation but also for convenience. Why bend unnecessarily?

It is a good idea to treat the timber to lengthen its life. Ideally do not use timber which has been treated with chemicals. The chemicals used are unkind to worms and may kill off your investment. But if you must use chemically-treated timber, seal it to prevent contact with worms. Hot paraffin wax is ideal but an easier preparation to use is a thinned down grafting compound made by Mobil Oil. Non-toxic to worms, it has other garden uses.

Indoor pits are also a convenient way of disposing of kitchen wastes, which are an excellent source of food for worms. Bury the waste beneath the bedding where the worms will soon dispose of it, leaving no trace of odours. However, don't rely solely on kitchen waste for the food supply. Add a little poultry mash or other ground grain occasionally but only sufficient to be eaten in a short time, otherwise it may sour.

Outdoor Pits

Beds in contact with the soil have the following advantages:

- Excess liquid and salts leach away naturally.
- The worms can retreat from heat or decaying food.
- The worms have access to fine grit for grinding food in the gizzard.
- Micro-organisms and bacteria in the soil can assist in breaking down organic wastes.

Outdoor pits may be made of anything that provides adequate drainage. While worms can live temporarily in excess water, they will leave home if the condition is permanent. Otherwise, they will eventually die.

Materials for outdoor pits include concrete blocks, hollow tiles, bricks or rough timber. Old stock water tanks, partly buried, oil drums cut in half, or any large metal containers make good pits.

Temporary pits may be made with bales of hay or straw but as the straw begins to rot down, the worms will work their way into the bales. However they are quite suitable if you are only going to breed worms seasonally, for example in a school project. When no longer needed, tear the bales apart, remove the worms and add the hay or straw to the bedding or compost heap. Small amounts of manure added to the hay makes excellent bedding.

For practicality, rectangular pits should not be much more than a metre wide, making the pit accessible from either side. The length can be fitted to space or materials available, from 2 to 30 metres or more. Medium sized pits are easier to work with, but long pits are manageable if partitioned into shorter segments, from say 2 to 3 metres. Work the pits in rotation when filling orders. A 1 x 7 metre pit should hold 50 000 to 60 000 mature worms. With several turnovers per year it should yield at least 200 000 worms annually.

A low-cost pit can be built by digging a hole, and smoothing the sides and bottom before lining the pit with galvanised metal mesh fastened to the walls with galvanised metal rods. Plaster about 3 cm of dampened plain river sand and cement over the walls and bottom. A layer of mixed coarse sand and gravel will keep the worms in and allow for drainage of excess water. Personally I don't like this pit as the worms tend to burrow down and make life difficult, but it is cheap.

If building with concrete blocks, a three-block pit is deep enough and easy to work. Keep one block above ground level to keep out surface water.

Generally worms seem to do best in wooden pits. Although timber is less durable and some worms may be lost through crawling, they are inexpensive to build and can be replaced when necessary.

Whatever the material, adequate drainage is essential. Agricultural drainage pipe set into at least 75–l00 cm of gravel is suitable, or else lay l0 cm of coarse sand and gravel, or crushed limestone in the bottom. Lay a covering of boards over this, about 1.5 cm apart, so you don't 'dig the gravel' when renewing bedding.

Protect the pit from weather and other predators. Lay a framework of boards at regular intervals, then cover with lengths of building paper, hessian, shadecloth, sacks, carpet, or corrugated iron, a few centimetres wider than the pit. The covering material will need to be weighted to keep it from blowing off and overlapped to keep out water. Remove the covers only for feeding, watering or working the pits.

Load the pit with about 30 cm of bedding and plant with about 100 to 200 breeders per square foot of bed surface area, or 500 to 1000 pit-run worms. When the worms have disappeared, wet the bedding, cover, and leave a few days. Once the worms have settled, feed them. Sprinkle water over the surface to keep the bedding moist but not wet. Don't flood it. Water should be rationed and covers must be provided in areas which experience heavy or prolonged rainfall. Water only when examination shows it is needed.

Initially placing a shallow layer of bedding means you will have plenty of room to add new layers of compost to provide new food and bedding for the breeders.

Protection for outdoor pits
Outdoor pits need protection from wind, excessive rain and sun. If you have trees or shade available build the pits there. If you have no natural shade or screening think about adding some kind of roof. A

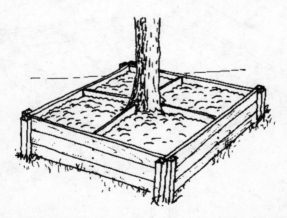

A worm bed built beneath a tree to utilise the shade

rough pole shed with a metal, board or slat roof will do the job. A split timber structure covered with chicken wire and shade cloth can also be used. This allows rain water to drip through but keeps the pits or bins shaded and cool in summer.

Another way to cover pits without building a roof is to build frames over the pits and cover with heavy polythene. If using polythene or glass, the pits need to be shaded artificially in hot weather.

Raised Beds

Mound beds can be built above the ground without framing the sides. Make the beds 1 m wide, 2 m high, and 1 m apart. Ensure that the beds have good drainage and check where the prevailing wind blows. Mulch with straw. The beds should be divided every 60 to 90 days.

Mound beds can be used successfully where there are huge amounts of garden waste or rubbish to be composted. Fill the furrows between the mounds with rubbish, and as it cools down, the worms can enter

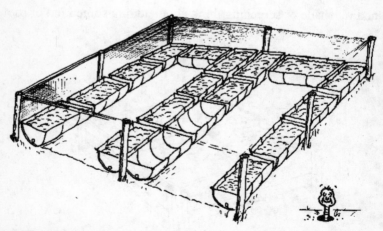

Each half-drum in this backyard mini worm farm (3 x 5 metres) layout can contain up to 10 000 worms

it from their bedding. After three to four months remove the original beds, sieve the material and sell the compost. Repeat the process, this time using the original furrows to hold the rubbish.

My way of dealing with a worm population explosion was by buying inexpensive oil drums for use as worm bodes and adding to them as required. I used metal drums, but the large plastic drums now available are just as hospitable and are lighter to handle.

Cut lengthwise, the edges filed off and covered with cut hose, and filled with bedding, they made comfortable bodes for up to 10 000 worms per bin. The bins were painted with Mobil Grafting Compound. An area, 3 x 5 metres, covered with a tacky but adequate roof contained 14 bins and meant I could deal with them even when it was raining. (Lucky me!)

The drums were raised off the ground and rested on wooden cradles. This enabled me to sit on my low stool by each drum and count worms. Covers were pieces of pre-loved corrugated iron weighted with heavy bits of concrete or blocks of wood.

Worm Bodes in the City

Flat dwellers can have a small worm bode on the balcony to dispose of kitchen waste and to provide wonderful inexpensive compost.

A 60 cm x 60 cm wooden box or a 40-litre rubbish bin are both suitable containers, but other possibilities could be old stainless steel or enamel sinks. Drill or punch nail holes in the bottom for drainage and place a drip tray underneath. Site the worm farm in a shaded and sheltered position. Layer the bottom of the container with 15 cm of bedding so the worms can retreat from strong food if they need to. Don't overfeed. Use the drip tray contents diluted as a liquid manure feed for plants.

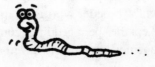

Bed & Breakfast

Bedding

Bedding is the home and shelter of the earthworm, the medium in which they live and breed. Good bedding should be moisture retentive, remain porous and crumbly, not pack tightly, and form part of the worms' food. To test, squeeze bedding material gently in your hand. It should cling together damply but not more than a few drops of liquid should drip out.

Aeration is important for healthy worms and to help prevent acid forming in the bins. Holes, which are 2 or 3 cm in diameter, may be cut in the bottom of a bin and screen mesh cut to fit the inside of the bin bottom. A rolled 3 cm tube of fine screen mesh, as long as the bin and extending through holes in the end of the box, and fastened all round, is a simple way of airing the bedding.

Bedding should be changed at least once a year, more frequently if production is heavy and the worm population high. As soon as it begins to pack tightly it should be changed.

Some breeders change bedding by dividing in half, removing spent bedding and the worms therein and replacing with fresh material. The half removed goes into new beds or bins, and is mixed with new material.

Others replace bedding during the 'high' worm selling season by removing and selling all the worms in each pit or bin, then taking all the material from the pit, replacing it with fresh bedding and restocking with new breeder worms. Some sell worms and bedding together. I have kept the spent bedding (compost and castings), waited until any egg capsules have hatched, removed the baby worms and then used the compost, but you will need to work out whether the time taken for this, both in weeks waiting and hours sorting, is worth it. I would be inclined to sell the compost and the egg capsules together.

Pits stocked lightly will produce larger worms, and more baby worms per breeder than heavily stocked pits. The ratio of worms per cubic foot has a direct bearing on their size and quality. One hundred worms with a cubic foot of bedding to themselves will grow faster and become larger. The average garden, with rich loam contains no more than 100 worms per cubic foot. A well stocked bed of commercial earthworms should contain at least 3000 worms of all sizes per cubic foot.

When preparing bedding mixtures, be flexible and use the material available. Look around for waste products and remember to test the pH. If you live near stables you may be able to get cheap horse box hay and manure from mucking out (but never when the horses have just been wormed). If you live near a pig farm you might get cheap pig farm slurry, some chicken manure from local hatcheries (but not too much because the manure is acidic), rabbit manure if there's a local rabbit farm, and vegetable waste from the local market gardens.

Bedding mixtures

An almost perfect basic compost or bedding, with a pH of about 7, would be a 50:50 mixture of manure and peat moss—the manure to provide a supply of food, and the peat moss to keep the bedding loose and to hold the moisture the worms need.

When mixing manure and peat moss, pre-soak the peat moss in water for at least 24 hours to thoroughly impregnate the fibres and keep the compost damp. The mixture should be thoroughly and evenly moistened but not soggy.

To this basic mixture, add crushed and finely chopped leaves and grass clippings, weeds or flower stalks, and waste materials from fish or poultry factories, breweries, groceries or food processors.

You can also add kitchen wastes: old bread, vegetable peelings, fruit skins, melon rinds, meat trimmings, sour milk, home-brew sediment . . . even dish water. Add lime to sweeten the mixture and prevent acids forming.

Manure

Aged or cold animal manure with a ratio of undigested grasses, straws and husks makes excellent bedding. Aged manure is manure that has already heated, and is not likely to heat up again. Green, or fresh, manure is rich, with salts too concentrated for worms and needs either aging (heating and cooling), or leaching (soaking and rinsing).

Aging manure

Green manure can be used in pits by adding about 33% by volume of crushed dead leaves, untreated sawdust or aged manure, and/or 15% by volume of peat moss. After the mixture has been thoroughly wetted and mixed, toss and work it and leave it to heat.

Once it begins to ferment, released gasses produce heat which may reach $75°C$, so it should not be disturbed during the first three days. After the three days, work the material again and add water if moisture has evaporated during the heating process.

Once heating has peaked, laying mash, corn meal, rolled oats, barley or other rolled or ground grain can be mixed in the proportion of two kilograms of grain plus one kilogram of lime (calcium carbonate) for each cubic metre of bedding.

After the grain has been added and heating completed, the bedding will be ready in around 10 days, but it will take longer in cool weather because the heating rate is slower. Larger masses of bedding may take up to a month, but frequent working, mixing and watering, piling in heaps in the pit and watering again, will hasten the process.

Leaching manure

To leach fresh manure, fill a bin or barrow with manure, cover with water and soak overnight, or flush the pile through several times. Strain off the liquid (which makes an ideal liquid fertiliser for plants), and crumble the manure.

If you can't use manure, ground or shredded paper, or corrugated paper boxes and cartons (containing glue which worms love) mixed with peat moss makes excellent bedding material. Charcoal and crushed oyster shell is useful in small quantities, but do not add builders' lime, wood ash, or any alkali.

Chopped hay, crushed corn cobs, chopped pea straw, bean vines, or almost any green material in small pieces, may be substituted for peat moss as an additive to either green or aged manure. Crushed leaves and untreated sawdust can be used but always add lime to neutralise acids.

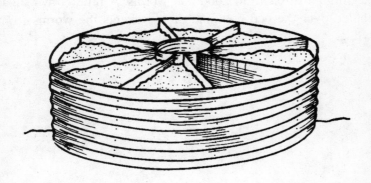

Farm Organic Converter. This eight-wedged tank-type container, constructed from metal or concrete, is suitable for large landholders. It works on a rotating principle with eight instead of three sections. It utilises offal, hides, hooves, hair, dags, as well as usual organic material. The centre cavity is for bone.

   Bury offal under several centimetres of soil or decomposing material.

   It is important to always leave one segment clear between the oldest and freshest composting material for ease of access or removal.

Stockyard wastes like hides, hair, guts, manure, hoofs and horns may be used as bedding and food material, but preferably not if you live in the city and want to remain friendly with your neighbours.

Amounts sufficient for small, inside breeder bins or tubs will complete the heating process in a day or two. Worms introduced before heating is completed will either die or migrate.

To test the bedding before adding worms, fill a small bucket or box with 15 cm of damp bedding and introduce 20 adult worms. If they are all alive and kicking after 24 hours, use the bedding. If they look sick, have died, or have migrated, it may need to be combined with some other product to make it palatable. Perhaps it needs another rinse. It's also a good idea to check the pH.

Once the worms have been established, top-feed or bury food in shallow trenches in one section of the bed. Food may be finely ground grain feeds such as poultry mash, calf meal, pulverised corn, cotton seed meal or similar products. These can be the additives that add size, girth and strength to good bait worms. A little brown sugar sprinkled over the bed now and then prevents the worms from crawling.

Gourmet Delicacies

Food means anything organic, often mixed to approach pH7. Dry foods include produce dusts, grains and flour sweepings. Wet foods include garbage, manures, slurry, sewage sludge and vegetables. Worms cannot eat any kind of food in its dry state, so all of these foods—regardless of whether they are classified as 'wet' or 'dry'—must be dampened before the worms can ingest them.

Grain feeds should be finely ground but be very careful not to mix these into the bedding. I found, to my cost, that using grain feed incorrectly caused a full bin of worms and bedding to become sour and mouldy. Sprinkle the grain in a thin layer on top of only one section of bedding and sprinkle with water to allow easy absorption, or scoop out a shallow trench and put the feed there. Remove uneaten food after three or four days.

Worms should be fed often and in small quantities. It is better to feed lightly every day or two, lightly spraying with water after feeding, than to feed a huge quantity once every ten days.

Poultry laying mash is good feed, but always use the cheapest and most readily available grain or mixture, such as rolled or ground oats and corn meal, wheat bran and corn meal, or soy bean meal with rabbit manure. Small amounts of lard or chopped suet may be mixed with grain feed occasionally.

I have found that fresh fish guts, scallop frills and freshly killed rats, courtesy of my cat, are considered to be a real treat. Check after a couple of days, especially in summer, to see that blowflies are not making free with the delicacies. At the slightest sign of maggots, clean out the bed.

Even dog food can be fed to the worms, although kibbled dog

foods and biscuits should be crushed and soaked in water before feeding.

You can also whet the earthworms' appetite by feeding chopped leaves of Asiatic comfrey.

Controlling acidity

In their natural habitat earthworms live happily in any old manure pile, compost heap, rubbish dump, or decaying vegetable or animal waste as long as the conditions are not too acidic. The same principle applies in pits, beds or bins.

You will soon learn to detect acidity in beds, particularly if you are adept at recognising changes in the worms' behaviour. They may become sluggish, tend to congregate in only one section of the bed, or have a decreased appetite. One of the earliest warning signals of problems with acidity is an increase in the number of nematode worms—minute white worms which can be mistaken for baby earthworms. Like slaters, they are not harmful to the earthworms but they are an indication that the bed is too acid. This may be corrected by the addition of lime sprinkled on food and bedding.

If absolutely essential the vet can be called and an antibiotic applied but should things reach this stage, most of the worms will have left in disgust. I'd be inclined to remove the remaining worms and start afresh. Incorporate the old bedding into the compost pile, being sure to add a decent dollop of lime.

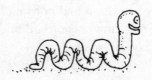

Introducing Worms
to the Beds

Once the bins, pits or beds are ready, and bedding and food is available, the worms can be introduced to their new home.

Start with mature breeders, pit-run mixed sizes, or small worms. Mature breeders will work faster, although if you're buying stock, pit-run should be cheaper and may well be an advantage because the young worms will adapt more readily to their new environment. Pit-run worms will probably take between 30 to 60 days to reach maturity.

When your stock arrives the worms will probably be balled up in a solid mass. Dump them on top of the prepared bedding, disentangle them and spread them over the surface. Make a few holes for them if you like but they'll probably disappear within a couple of minutes, especially if it's sunny or you have an electric light over the bin because light irrititate the worms' elementary nervous system. They may be inactive for a few days but will soon begin feeding and breeding if conditions and temperatures are favourable.

Try to overcome any desire you may have to poke and prod the bed to see how the worms are settling down. They need time to get used to their new home without being disturbed.

Speeding Up Production

Propagation Boxes

A dozen boxes of breeding worms are useful not only to breed worms rapidly but also to become more closely acquainted with the habits and breeding of earthworms and to correct any errors in feeding.

Under the high concentration of breeders in boxes, egg capsule production reaches its peak and probably produces more worms per cubic foot of compost than any other method.

Boxes should be small enough to handle easily, uniform in size for stacking and have handles to move them easily. They should be tightly constructed but have small holes in the bottom for drainage.

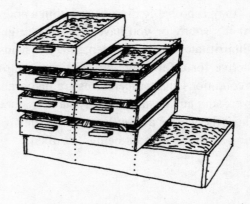

Stack breeder boxes for space utilisation and convenience. A moderate temperature and pH controlled bedding are needed.

Dividers between the boxes help air circulation. Stack the boxes off the floor to prevent worms from working their way out through the drain holes or cracks. Shadecloth or hessian cut larger than the box is a good idea to help the damp bedding come away easily when the box is removed.

Label and date each box, including information such as worm type, when bedded, type of bedding, feed, and when the first breeders were removed.

Compare the results from different boxes by noting the number of worms removed.

Breeder boxes may be stacked in a garage, cellar, basement, attic or spare room where they will be protected from freezing temperatures or excessive heat. A basement is best for inside worm propagation as the temperatures will most likely remain constant, or if necessary you can control the heat .

The bedding material can be the same as that used for pits, but again remember to check the pH. My one major worm farming disaster occurred when I thoughtfully provided the big breeders in several propagation boxes with tasty and warm bedding consisting of sheep dags and straw. Tasty it may have been, but it was certainly too acid and all the worms 'walked'. I hadn't tested the bedding first. When I did (after the event) the pH was far too acid. Fortunately I only lost 5000 breeders, but if I had filled the oil drums with the acid bedding I would have lost thousands and thousands of earthworms through my own fault.

Making the bed

In the bottom of each box spread a layer or two of shadecloth, hessian, straw, dry leaves or newspapers to help drainage and provide supplementary worm food. Fill the box two-thirds with damp bedding and on top of that, dump about 500 breeders. In a few minutes they will burrow down out of sight. Spread a thin layer of poultry mash on top of the bedding and water lightly. Cover the surface with wet hessian or carpet to prevent the contents from drying out.

Except for an occasional feeding and sprinkling through the hessian covering, it needs no further care for 21 to 30 days, when the contents of the box should be ready to dump and divide (if the breeders are mature).

Dumping and dividing

Dump the contents of the breeding box on top of a smooth table, rake with the fingers into a cone-shaped pile and let stand for a short time in bright light so the mature worms will work down to the bottom of the pile. Little by little, transfer the compost with its egg capsules and baby worms back into the original box, removing any mature worms that might be found.

Have a new box ready with fresh compost. Put the mature breeders in it, add food, cover with hessian and sprinkle as in the first operation. That box should be ready to dump and divide in another 21 to 30 days.

The box of capsules and young worms may remain undisturbed, except for occasional feeding and watering, for about 90 days, when it should be full of young worms hatched from the capsules, plus some that have developed to breeder size, indicated by the band or clitellum. If the box seems to be crowded, dump and divide it, again transferring the compost and small worms back into the original box and preparing a new box for the breeders, which will then take their place in the 21–30 day rotation.

Continuous production

Breeder worms should be removed from the culture boxes when the first hatch of young worms are about half grown. As soon as the first generation of young worms begins to deposit capsules they should be removed. In this way, continuous production may be had until the bedding is completely worked out.

Prepare the outdoor pits while the worms are multiplying in these low cost beds. By the time the large pits are ready and filled with bedding, you'll have plenty of good worms for stocking them.

Egg Capsules on Demand

Although the average 'hatch' from an egg capsule is about five baby worms, a capsule may contain up to 20. The number depends on the breeders' health and maturity.

Egg capsules are an ideal way to introduce worms to gardens, orchards, pasture, pot plants and herb boxes, but be sure they are the correct species for the environment. They are inexpensive to mail, and will stand more rugged conditions of climate and travel than worms. They store dormant at 5°C and only hatch above 10°C. Worms acclimatise easily with this method. They will soon hatch out under the damp mulch and colonise their new bodes .

Where space is at a premium, egg capsule production can be profitable. In any case, mature breeders like an occasional holiday or change of scene away from the bed, and it can stimulate egg production.

Your normal propagation boxes can be utilised for egg capsule production. Stack the boxes in a temperature not lower than 10°C and not higher than 27°C.

Soak hessian, sacks or dense shadecloth in water for 24 hours, and place in the box in about five or six layers.

Lightly sprinkle in between each layer with a teaspoonful of finely ground grains mixed with a pinch of lime to each cupful of grain. Dampen well, cover, check the pH and when around 25°C or below, introduce 25 breeders per layer.

Every 10 days shake the worms and capsules from the hessian, remembering not to handle the capsules without gloves as oils from fingers touching the capsules may cause mould and infertility. Store the capsules carefully in cool temperatures. Place the worms between the layers with a further sprinkling of food.

Post or courier the capsules in between damp cotton wool or damp peat moss with a clear instruction sheet about the hatching temperature, and their need for moisture and shelter under mulch on damp soil, and so on.

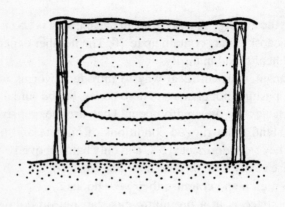

Layering for concentrated egg capsule production

Fat Toughies for Fishing

If you need quantity for the garden, then you need quality for fishing. This means the worms used as bait should be large, fat and hard.

A special fattening pit should be built, as fat worms do not breed well and newly hatched worms do not thrive in soggy, heavily fed fattening pits. The fattening pit supplies the biggest worms with the kind of feed needed. Unless you intend selling worms for bait, fatten 200 at a time for your own fish bait needs, although the rules and conditions are the same whether fattening 300 or 3000. The mature worms should be fattened in uncrowded conditions as an overfull fattening pit inhibits maximum growth.

The pit or bin should be deeper than the usual breeder pits and have plenty of shade. Suitable bedding materials are soaked peat moss, coffee grounds and shredded paper. The coconut fibre used for lining plant baskets is also ideal for this purpose. Do not keep the bedding too wet or the worms will be too soft.

Sewage sludge, allowed to air dry for a year before using, is ideal for fattening, especially with a thin layer of horse manure added. Food of high grain content also makes worms solid, muscled and excellent for fishing. Barley is probably best as long as it is very fine. Pollard and bran are also good and ordinary wheat flour or cornflour is excellent if you can afford to feed them with it.

A good mix of grains to fatten worms is 50% of poultry pellets with 10% each of wheat or cornflour, powdered milk, bran and lime. Measure the ingredients, add water to cover, plus another 50% of water. Soak the feed for at least an hour, stirring occasionally. If the mixture is not extremely sloppy, add more water.

Feeding should be done weekly, feeding only as much as the worms will consume. Place the feed in a strip across the surface and cover lightly with bedding material. The worms will quickly adjust to taking food from this particular spot which will make harvesting easier. Cover the bin with wet hessian or shadecloth.

The high quality of food tends to encourage acidity so it's a good idea to add lime every time you feed. It can be added to the food in the proportion of 10% of weight, but if nematodes appear this level should be increased.

Harvesting

Picking the beds clean

If the objective is to send high quality, graded worms to your customers, then the packaged worms should be free of any active organic matter that is not placed there for a specific purpose. This means that unless they are being packed and sent in compost they should be free of any bedding or feed.

Depending on the bedding, the type of worm, and the food, preparations for harvesting should begin some time before picking worms from the bed.

Worms can be removed faster if the bedding is slightly drier than normal. Water lightly and only if necessary, at least one day in advance. Red worms grown in deep beds with heavy organic material like manure have a lower rate of evaporation, so not watering for several days in advance may be an option.

Reduce watering

During hot weather, when most worms are picked and the bedding is (ideally) loose and fluffy from much digging and stirring, reducing the amount of water encourages the worms to spread out rather than collect in masses around feed and moisture. This makes it easier for pickers to sort and grade as the worms are uncovered.

Once worms have been exposed and have crawled back under cover, it may be difficult to find them again until the bedding has been watered, the worms fed, and they have collected at their normal depth.

Pickers seldom find more than 20% to 30% of the total worms available in one picking, although this means the same bed can produce worms for removal every few days rather than for only one or two crops in a season.

Reduce feeding

Feed should also be reduced two days before any scheduled picking. If manure is used, enough time should pass to allow the worms to clean it up before they are picked. In the case of dry feed and ground grains, timing is less important, but they should be fed only lightly the day before picking. This is not only to avoid picking up feed along with worms, but also to avoid mixing the feed into the bedding.

Red worms should not be picked too often. Infrequent harvesting allows better development of both older and younger worms, and results in heavier, livelier worms. Beds picked too often will reduce the population to small young worms popularly called 'bedruns'. On average, providing the worm has had sufficient food, water and good bedding, the older it is, the larger it is.

Harvesting and grading

Short of removing worms and bedding together, the best way to remove worms from the beds is by uncovering them with a short-handled light garden fork. The worms are placed in a container or cup, and graded and counted until the desired number has been counted. Although counting and weighing the first thousand will give a legal count acceptable in the pit or bedrun trade, counting all the harvested worms is the best way to grade if you are selling large handpicked bait or breeders.

Pickers become amazingly adept and can grade 2000 to 3000 worms per hour—more, if a bed is heavily populated.

After the worms have been placed in the containers do not leave them in sunny spots or exposed to rain. Take them to the packing area which should be well lit because worms will try to bury themselves in the presence of bright light. As they burrow downwards, the dirt and bedding picked up along with the worms is pushed to the surface of the container, from where it is easily removed. This makes the worms cleaner and easier to pack.

If individual grading is not the objective of harvesting, it is not necessary to reduce the feed or water beforehand. If you are harvesting a large ground bed, a long-handled, closely tined manure fork is a good tool. A single forkful may bring up as many as 1500 mature worms at a time.

If the objective is to divide the beds, or to sell the worms by weight rather than grade, feeding them a few hours before harvesting will make the job easier because they will all concentrate around the feed area.

If the worms are numerous and the bedding is not packed, fork the bedding including worms into a wheelbarrow and leave it in the sun or a well-lit room for 5 to 10 minutes. The worms will burrow down away from the light. Gently skim off the bedding down to where the worms are. Repeat the process every few minutes until only worms are left.

Another way to harvest earthworms is to work on benches or tables of convenient height, barrowing worm-filled compost from the pit to the table. Large shallow trays may also be used and as each tray containing several hundred worms is emptied, it is refilled or replaced with another tray.

If the worms are being packaged for fish bait, count them directly into the containers, in 25s, 50s etc. If you are filling bulk orders of mixed grades, save yourself the tiresome and repetitive problem of counting worms by using a weighing method. A reasonable quality scale divided by gram weight is necessary.

First of all, count several thousand worms by hand and grade them into breeders, and so on, in thousand lots. The standard practice is to add one hundred to account for any deaths or disasters. Weigh these worms and mark their weight in grams on the side of the scales. Any time in the future that you want to count worms of this size, simply grade and pile onto the scale until the number of grams registered with the first count is reached. Don't forget to add the weight of the container to the exercise.

The same method may be applied to all grades or types of worms, bed or pit-run, breeders or bait worms, if the objective is to save time and labour costs. However, if the worms vary considerably in size from one month to the next, count a batch every so often to be sure of giving a good count and yet not too generous an overcount. Larger worms will arrive at a short count while smaller worms will give a large overcount. While your customers may not always count their order, you don't want to explain to them why the number is short.

If you are charging top prices for top quality breeders however, handpicking and counting is the quality way to go.

Storing Worms

If you live in a very cold part of the country where breeding almost ceases in winter, store the breeders in old wash tubs or half barrels and take a winter holiday. If you're a commercial breeder, ten tubs will get you off to a good start in the spring.

The tub sides should be tight, although there should be several small drainage holes in the bottom. Half fill the tub with damp aged manure, and put 8–10 cm of dried sewage sludge on top.

Put 6000 breeder worms in this and let them settle for a day or two. Spread an 8 cm layer of wet clay over the worms without pressing or compacting. Smooth as much as possible.

Store the worms at 5°C (certainly no higher than 10°C) and forget them for four months. When you remove them the earthworms will be much smaller, very dark in colour and quite lifeless. Once replaced into fresh bedding, they will recover their spirits, colour, size and appetites, and having wintered over, will be ready to breed with renewed vigour.

Packing and Moving House

Packing Materials

Lightweight peat or sphagnum moss is the best packaging material. Add water at least 24 hours before the peat is used and squeeze hard enough so that a handful will surrender no more than a few drops of water. This should sustain the worms, even over a long journey.

Break up and presoak the peat in a large tub, tank, or half barrel with water, using a ratio of 1 part water to 2 parts peat.

When worms are placed into a package with limited space they begin an aimless wandering until they find the most comfortable part of the container, which will depend on the package temperature, humidity and movement of air. If it is very hot, the worms will try to come to the surface. If it is cool, the worms will find a comfortable place on or near the bottom of the container. In very cool or cold conditions, the worms will probably form a mass at the centre.

For bulk packaging (1000 worms or more), the container should have about 3 cm of barely damp peat moss placed in the bottom. Place 100 or so thoroughly cleaned worms, then another measure of peat, another helping of worms and so on until the package contains 1000 worms, plus the overcount.

Tightly packed peat prevents circulation of available air as well as restricting worm movement. Never pack the peat in firmly or bounce the package to settle the material. The same applies for compost.

Packaging materials

Packaging from many industries will be satisfactory for worms, providing air and moisture are available. The exception is plastic bags which may cause condensation in which the worms drown. Many large breeders in the USA and Australia use standard sized waxed ice cream or milk cartons.

Some use plastic ice cream containers with air holes punched in the lids. Even cardboard cartons, lined with aluminium foil, are okay. The main thing is that the material be damp enough to preserve the worms and that they have access to air without being able to escape from the container.

When it is available, worms use more oxygen per pound than people, and become lively and colourful. As the oxygen in any container is depleted, they become less active and their skin turns dark.

Do not put too many worms in the package because worms are often damaged by their own weight. They will also arrive in better condition if they are not crowded.

When the necessary number of worms and peat moss or compost has been added, leave a small space between the top of the peat moss and top of the container to allow a small amount of internal evaporation and movement of air without condensation forming.

The worms must be packaged in a way that will overcome careless handling by postal staff.

Providing they are thoughtfully packed, worms will travel and store well in cool temperatures. Tests have indicated that worms can be stored 120 days and more without harm to either worm or package, provided their environmental demands are met.

Remember that any carton, crate or box that is used as a worm container must be well ventilated. If custom cartons are purchased, ask the manufacturer to cut four slits, two in each side of the box. To preserve structural strength, make vertical 3 cm wide and about 8 cm long slits. Make your own slits in salvaged cartons with a sharp knife or poke about ten holes at each end with a metal skewer.

Marking packages

All packages should be marked LIVE EARTHWORMS! DO NOT EXPOSE TO EXTREME HEAT OR COLD! PLEASE DELIVER PROMPTLY! Make sure you include the phone number, return address and an instruction leaflet.

It is not necessary to add worm food to the packed worms, but if you consider the journey long and arduous, put a small amount of fine corn meal, chicken mash or rolled oats on the top of each package.

If sending egg capsules by post, pack in damp cottonwool in padded bags and send Expresspost.

Package Conditioning

Worms in lower temperatures tend to remain inactive. They eat less, therefore loss of conditioning is less likely to occur through lack of food. Their pores close, preventing moisture loss through evaporation, and they may absorb water from the damp peat surrounding them. Their length is generally reduced by about 10% with a corresponding expansion of diameter.

A cool worm needs less oxygen and emits less carbon dioxide. Worm fanciers consigning large quantities of earthworms can undertake some simple procedures to prepare worms for warm temperatures and probable lack of sufficient oxygen in transit.

Pick, package, label and seal the worms in the carton or container. Place it in a cool room in which the temperature is maintained at 15°C to 20°C. This allows the carton, package, packaging material, and worms to be cooled, and depending on environmental conditions, it will remain cool for some time. Red worms can be conditioned at a temperature of 10°C or 15°C. Small growers may achieve this by placing the packed and sealed goods in a refrigerator on the lowest setting for 5 to 10 hours. Large growers might consider building a small coolroom.

Once the consignment is on its way and the peat moss warms, the worms begin to move about and will arrive with a healthy appetite. This can sometimes cause them to double in size and weight in three to seven days.

The reduction of temperature seems to give the worms a real boost of energy. Their appetite improves, their sexual activity increases, and a general quickening of all their reactions is noted.

What the Buyer Needs to Know

Regardless of the quantity of worms delivered, they should be cared for immediately upon arrival. If they have not been conditioned by a lowering of their body temperature, the worms may be hot and agitated from vibration and travel. Almost certainly they will have had insufficient air along the way, and most probably the moisture in the packaging material has evaporated so that the worm is now losing its body liquids to the dry bedding and air.

Customers should be told, preferably in advance, that all worms are susceptible to heat and dehydration and that proper care should be exercised in their preservation.

Fortunately, worms are able to exist and even maintain a large degree of vitality for several days without food, but not without air and water. The skin condition and colour depends on water, as does the proper absorption of oxygen. Without skin tone, a worm is dying. So it is up to the purchaser to add both food and water at his end, the sooner the better after the worms arrive.

Enemies of Worms

Earthworms' enemies are centipedes, ants, rats, mice, mites and birds, and these must be excluded from the beds or destroyed. Worms like a neutral situation; fortunately for the worms, most harmful insects prefer acid conditions.

Beds can be treated after the worms are installed by using an insecticide spray which will help prevent the reproduction of unwanted pests. The worms may be sluggish for a day or two but will not be harmed.

In small operations cover the beds with frames or mesh screens. Mice love to nest in outdoor pits (and raised oil drums), and the best cure for rats and mice, if a good pussy cat is not available, is rat poison around the pits.

Centipedes are vicious and can take a heavy toll on young worms. They are attracted to acid beds so check the pH. If they are only occasional invaders, catch them when you see them. Otherwise, spray the area before the beds are constructed.

Ants remove starches and sugars from the bedding and feed. As a consequence the worms suffer and do not grow or deposit capsules as they should. Ants may also carry away the capsules. Feeding below the surface, a neutral pH, damp beds, and changing the food to raw vegetable waste may solve the problem. Boiling water can be used to destroy the ant nest if it can be traced. Try these methods before dusting the floor around the outside of the pits with pyrethrum. Do not get it in the pits as it will kill the earthworms. Any poisons that kill ants will kill worms!

Like ants, mites like sweet food. Control mites by spraying with any household insect spray, but do not feed or water for a few days after spraying.

Although kerosene is an old-fashioned remedy, it is useful in providing barriers to insects. Strings of twine or yarn, soaked in kerosene and tied around the legs of bins, or attached to the outsides of boards will prevent many pests and insects from entering the beds. I've also heard that some growers put the legs of raised beds into cans of water and kerosene.

Pesticides, weedicides, poisons, fertilisers and other chemicals are all bad news for worms. Where possible use less harmful alternatives like garlic or rhubarb leaf sprays, companion planting, pH adjustment, mulching, green manuring, chisel ploughing, sheet composting, slashing and strip cropping. Also encourage useful predatory insects like ladybirds and mantids.

Alcohol from rancid sweet food can sicken worms, so be careful if adding old fruit pulp to the bed. Add limestone to correct the pH, water well, aerate the beds, and reduce feeding for a few days.

Lateral Marketing

To market earthworms successfully you need to open your mind and think laterally to make the most out of any available or potential markets.

Quite apart from obvious ones like mail order, local gardeners, aquariums and bird shops, you might have to work a little at getting across the message 'Worms Are Good For More Than Gardens!'

The best strategy is free publicity. Once you're at the stage where you have worms to sell, and are happy and confident about the practical results that worms produce, get in touch with local community papers to do a story on your worms and how they work. Other options and markets are listed below:

Home sales   Advertise locally, hold open days, and distribute leaflets to garden circles. Sell plants growing in castings in pots. Make sure you have plenty of worms and castings to sell.

Dairy farmers, pig breeders   Do some research into converting waste into compost. Set up a pilot scheme using slurry or cow shed tailings—it needn't be big. Gather a few figures—costs, time, output—and then make the farmer/breeder an offer he/she can't refuse (either to sell sufficient worms to convert the waste into a saleable product or for you to buy the slurry and convert it yourself).

Orchardists   Persuade an orchardist into letting you treat a sample tree. In twelve weeks the difference will be demonstrable. Invite groups of orchardists to see that it is healthier and producing greater quantities of fruit. In suburbia, offer the valuable service of rejuvenating old, sick or valuable trees.

Bird breeders, poultry farms (commercial and domestic units)   Set up a box or bin similar to the Garbage Guts Muncher to show how dead birds, feathers, etc. can be converted to saleable castings and to live worms which can be fed to poultry.

Fish breeders, trout hatcheries and eel farmers   Set up bin, box or pit systems to demonstrate fish bait production on a big scale. Trout hatcheries and eel farmers need plenty of worms.

Food processors and producers, restaurants and green grocers Show how worms will help them to convert their waste into profit.

Organic wastes   Be ambitious and approach the local sewage treatment plant. You could obtain samples and check and correct the pH. Separate the solids from liquids (strain, filter, and let the sediment settle), and capture nutrients in liquids by filtering through straw, sawdust, shredded paper/cardboard. Introduce worms, and test food and bedding and adjust until it is palatable.

Fishermen   Sell worms to fishing tackle shops, replacing the unsold stock every 7–14 days and returning them to the beds. Sell fattened worms in 'bait boxes' or portable bait carriers. Advertise in fishing magazines or by letters to clubs. Take a van and chilled bins of bait worms to fishing contests and sell on the spot.

Councils in small country towns   Convince the council that worms can be used to convert all the organic waste in small country tips into compost to sell. Get householders to recycle their rubbish in the interests of the project.

Schools   Set up an educational project at the local school and sell sufficient worms to raise funds by selling compost to parents.

Agricultural field days   Set up a table with information sheets, worms, capsules, castings and be prepared to take big orders.

Garden centres   Approach garden centres and set up cooperative ventures to sell worms and castings in conjunction with seasonal happenings, such as rose days, first day of spring, etc.

Export The first person to crack the Japanese bait market for recreational fishing will be able to retire as a millionaire!

Compost enthusiasts, Garbage Guts customers, gardeners, balcony gardeners and fish breeders Sell bedding with capsules or worms by the bucket to these people.

In addition you will need good instruction sheets, care of worms inserts, price lists and order books, an imaginative printed label for shipping cartons, and some office supplies, such as letterheads and envelopes.

Earthworm Facts

- If you cut a worm in half, both ends do not regrow. It depends on where the cut is made as to whether it survives at all. If it is severed behind the clitellum, then the head part is capable of growing a new tail.
- They are larger than their ancestors due to evolution, feeding and care but have retained their toughness and liveliness, colouring and prolific breeding habits.
- They stay at home under normal conditions, and will not migrate or crawl away if adequate food and moisture is provided.
- They are adaptable to widely varying climatic and soil conditions and do well over a wide range of temperatures. They will live and multiply wherever moisture and organic foods are abundant.
- Each healthy earthworm, under favourable conditions, may produce an egg capsule every seven to ten days. These capsules incubate in 14 to 21 days, each hatching out from two to twenty worms, with an estimated average of five.
- The newly hatched worms will mature to breeding age, though not fully grown, in 60 to 90 days, as indicated by the formation of the clitellum, the thick muscular band about one-third the length of the worm from its head.
- Egg capsules will lie dormant or hatch more slowly if temperatures are too low or the beds are too dry. Capsules may be held dormant by refrigeration or drying, then hatched at a later date by restoring normal temperature and moisture conditions.

- The domesticated earthworm will continue to grow after it reaches the breeder stage for as much as six months or so before reaching its full size, and may be further fattened for bait by special feeding. The normal length for a fully matured and well fed red worm is about 7–9 cm; under special feeding it may reach 10 cm or more.

- Red worms make fine bait worms, and live and remain active for long periods under water.

- Red worms have a life span of several years (when protected); some biologists estimate as many as 10 to 15 years.

- An earthworm will swallow its own weight in soil or compost each 24 hours, and after extracting the food value will deposit a like weight in castings rich in plant foods.

- Earthworms will breed continuously under relatively constant temperatures if sufficient food and moisture are available (for example, in caves or in basements where temperatures range from $5^{\circ}C$ to $22^{\circ}C$). In their natural habitat breeding slows down or lapses in mid winter or in extreme summer heat.

- One active breeder, under favourable year-round food, moisture and temperature conditions, will produce approximately 50 to 60 capsules, which should hatch about 200 young earthworms. But the young earthworms themselves become breeders within three to four months from the capsule stage, resulting in a rapid pyramiding of production before a year has passed. A single breeder with its children and grandchildren may produce a total of 1000 to 1500 progeny within the twelve-month period.

- Fresh manure may be used in the beds if it is spread over the top of the pit where there is no danger of heating and where the worms may feed on it from the under side.

- Most worm fanciers do not feed their worms too many citrus fruits or skins as they are acidic. Worms don't like onion skins, eucalyptus or pepper leaves. Never feed leaves or grasses that have been treated with poison sprays. Avoid high concentrations of vinegar, salt or strong alkalies.

- Mature earthworms will suffer from abrupt changes in climate and environment but will gradually adapt. Worm fanciers should advise their customers on the use of bedding material similar to that in which the breeder stock has been reared. The young worms hatched from egg capsules, however, will rapidly adopt the soil and food conditions under which they are hatched.

What Have Earthworms Taught Me?

At the beginning of this booklet I stated that I set up my small earthworm farming experiment because I thought it a good money-making venture for a relative. After two years of breeding and studying the small creatures out of interest, I became convinced of it!

Earthworm breeding has the potential to earn a few farmers a substantial amount of money, and give a large number of people extra money to supplement their wages or benefit.

If I wanted to be the biggest breeder of earthworms in the country I would grow the worms indoors in tiered bins or removable racks, using a pulley system or a small forklift to slide out and/or lift the trays or bins of worms and bedding. An enormous number of worms could be grown, stacked in trays 10 to 12 high.

The advantages of an indoor farm like this are that you control the temperature, the light, the weather, the feeding and watering of the stock.

Defunct greenhouses, dairy factories, cowsheds, old barns or large sheds could be converted relatively simply. The large quantities of bedding needed would be made indoors as well, and you could set up a vibrating belt to separate the worms from bedding and grade at the same time. Tables for sorting and packing would also be easily accessible.

However, I am not going to become a big earthworm breeder because I have now sold my experimental earthworm farm to someone whom I believe will make a very good living from his investment.

You are entitled to ask why, if worm farming is such a money spinner, I am not going to continue breeding worms. The first and most important reason is that I am a writer not a worm farmer; hence this book. The second is that the physical demands—turning over bedding, lifting heavy bins, hefting propagation boxes, and so on—are too much for me.

Nevertheless, my experience with earthworms has taught me enough to know that I will always have at least one bin in operation, so there will always be sufficient hardworking earthworms happily converting my kitchen and garden waste into valuable compost and castings for the flower and vegetable gardens.

Bibliography and Recommended Reading

Appehof, M. (1982) *Worms Eat My Garbage*, Flower Press, Kalamazoo, USA

Buckerfield, J.C. (1994)' Management of appropriate earthworms for agriculture and vermiculture', Technical Report No 2/1994, CSIRO Division of Soils, Urbrae, South Australia

Darwin, C.(1881) *The Formation of Vegetable Mould, through the Action of Worms, with Observations on Their Habits*, Murray, UK

Douglas, D.E. and Gaddie, R.E. (1975) *Earthworms for Ecology and Profit, Vol. 1,* Bookworm Publishing Co., USA

Douglas, D.E. and Gaddie, R.E. (1977) *Earthworms for Ecology and Profit, Vol. 2,* Bookworm Publishing Co., USA

Handreck, K. and Lee, K. (1986) *Earthworms for Gardeners and Fishermen*, Discovering Soils No. 5, CSIRO, Melbourne, Australia

Lambert, D. (1983) E*arthworm Breeding for Profit: Practical Production and Marketing of Earthworms in Australia*, Weston & Co., Kiama, NSW

Morgan, C. (1969) *Profitable Earthworm Farming*

Morgan C. (1972) *Earthworm Selling & Shipping Guide*

Russell, E.J. (1959) *The World of the Soil*, Collins/Readers Union

Shields, E.B. (1982) *Raising Earthworms for Profit—a multi million dollar market*, Shield Publications, Wisconsin, USA

Sosnowski, J. and Sosnowski, S. (1982) *Earth Worms for the Peaceful Pleasures of Gardening and Fishing*, The Big Fat Worm Farm, Nambucca Heads, NSW

Index

packaging, 57, 59, 63
  area, 58
  material, 62, 64, 65
  temperature, 62
padded bags, 64
pasture improvement, 11, 21–3
pests, 66
pesticides, 15, 67
pH meter, 18
pickers, 57–8
potting mix, 21, 34
poultry mash, 51
problems, 66–7
propagation boxes, 16–17, 50–1
protection, from elements, 39

raised beds, 17, 40–1
rectangular pits, 38
Red worm, 23, 28–9, 57–8, 72
reproductive cycle, 25–7

sewage recycling, use of worms in, 17, 20, 47, 55, 61, 69
shade, 39
shade cloth, 32, 38, 40, 51, 53, 56
shredded paper, 12–13, 31, 45
soil, effect of worms on, 20–1
spent bedding, 42
storage of worms, 61
supplementary worm feed, 51

temporary pits, 37
temperature, 18, 64, 72
Tiger worm, *see* Manure worm
tools, 18

ventilation, 63

weighing worms, 59
worm bodes, 16, 35, 41
worms, types of, 11, 28–9,